68 Days

Emanjilli Marie

Presentation by *BookLeaf Publishing*

Web: www.bookleafpub.com

E-mail: info@bookleafpub.com

ISBN:9789357616782

First edition 2022

To 18 year old me

I'm sorry you were not seen or heard

We've got this now

*and we will not repeat the mistakes of the
past*

Spring

Sitting here watching as the weeks fly by,
Wondering if you're going to stay for awhile.
Sitting here watching all the leaves turn green.
Wondering if they're as delicate as they seem.

Spring spreads her love and all her warmth,
The trees, flowers and bees all start to buzz for
her.

See that cherry blossom looking oh so fine.
Everyday another petal joins the tribe.
Snow peas climbing up
Embracing her trunk.
Watching from my window
I feel slightly love drunk.

Thankyou Spring for all that you do.
I don't know where we'd be without you.

You bring all the colour and light with you.
We love breathing in everything that you do.
There's trails of joy wherever you move
As the breeze whispers through
We can all smell the amazing work that you do.

My Love

That is my woman there.
Standing Strong.
she has the biggest heart
you could ever dream of
because we are feminists
objectifying Her is wrong
but I can't stop
telling everyone
of how Amazing
she makes my world.

Psychiatric Inpatient Unit

IPU
Isolated Ill
In Iatrogenesis
Irreversible

Compulsory Treatment

Ensnared
Legally, Completely
Horrifying, Mortifying, Soul-destroying
Supposedly Helpful
Bewildering

The Bee Sting

Hope Swirling
Today's the day
IPU captive no more
Home to children.

SLAM!

Resentments, Accusations,
Different Narratives
Restrictions,
Institutionalisation,
Different, Other.

No gluten for 31 days.
Oh Hi besting, thanks for the comfort.
Creamy, sweet custard.
Crunchy, sticky almond.
Happy childhood memory.

Disastrous Decision!
cramp, cramp, cramp
shit, shit, shit

No welcome home
Pathetic Life Partner
Hope Stung and Now in Hiding.

Community

Connected
Thriving Together
Gardens, Markets, Music, Fun.
Finding Family

Detained Again

Detained in the psychiatric unit,
Cold walls, noxious smells, lifeless colours.
Heart aching with the separation from loved
ones.
Wife, Children - 1, 2, 3, 4.

Every morning at 5.55am
I clamber out of bed and sit
waiting for the 6am
opening of the doors

The hands on the clock reach 6 and 12
The nurse slips the key into it's keyway,
I hear the click
of Freedom

Outside I step.
Instant Comfort.

The fresh air kisses my skin,
so soft and crisp
the cool swirls in through my nose
and my chest rises
then puffs up my lungs
as I savour my second breath.

Kookaburra starts his morning cackle
creating waves of pleasure as they vibrate from
his perch
down to my ears.
The ancestors are happy.
I remember Nan's teaching ' when those
kookaburras laugh girl, they're happy for you'.

I continue my morning sensory diet as I stroll
around the brightly flowering spring garden;
bluebells, yellow calendula, pink cherry
blossom, green snowpeas, purple borage, white
daisies, red camellias.
Each beautiful colour balm for the soul as my
eyes drink in the different shapes, shades and
smells.

And the final hug of the morning reaching out to
feel the silky softness of the curry plants.

As I lean down to them and shake off the
morning dew my fingers are left tingling with
wet kisses from the final magical gift of the
morning.

White Lies

Look as they smile
While others cry
How can they think
Their actions are worthwhile

I watched the sun rise
At the breaking of the day
And I watched the sun set
Crimson with their blood

I need to keep striving for life
Looking for the kindness in all of humankind
I trusted Elders to guide my on my way
Throughout my journey
I'm sorry if I turned your hair grey.

While they brought in the grog
and they brought in the ice
and the gunja that grows there so well.
I brought in the sugar with my white privilege
and Now I can't see through the white lies.

And you can't see to stop
drinking the grog and taking the ice
and the gunja that turns your eyes red

I know they took her son,
and now she's gone
and her babies are left to cry.

Please keep striving for life
Keep finding goodness in those whitefella eyes.
You know who you can trust along the way.
You've been brought up right way.

I'm sorry we took your mothers away.

And we wonder why they bring in the grog
and bring in the ice,
and grow the gunja so well.
Some can't even see their white privilege
and just keep hiding behind white lies.

Still Locked Up

Dropping In,
I surrender my heart to you.
I'll even bring my smile with me too,
Especially for you.

Light ripples through,
The harsh, cold barriers of my enclosure.
Where I've been stripped raw
Again and again

I know they try
To look after me
Sometimes it's hard to remember
That they actually care about me
When I'm left all alone
In a cold, locked room.
No phonecalls or visitors,
to remind me of my life
Sometimes I can even forget, I have a wife.

And then I feel the soft clouds
Full of magic elixir.
As they leave your etheral hands
As you reach out to me.

My pain shifts
As you bewitch me with your love
Again and again,
and again and again.

I want seclusion rooms,
To transform into a refuge,
Where people are safe
and Free to rest
and Get a good feed.

Where darkness consumes light

When I called you the other night boy,
You heard it in my voice then.
I thought I needed your warmth
To get me through.

Bring the flowers you chose so tenderly.
Lay them down there beside me discreetly
And hold my hand for that instant
Where darkness consumes light.

In that moment,
I become so frightened
I need your touch to set me free.
People look at me.
They don't understand
How your love sets me on fire.

You threw love, not stones.
You shared kind smiles, not coins.
You gave your time to many,
And always respected me.

So many wounds and scars,
Seen, held, and finally put to rest.

Grey

Grey, miserable day
heart in mouth
hole in chest
tethered life-line fraying
more and more each second that passes

Fresh beginnings
new opportunities
at what cost?
to benefit who?

Find a new you
a positive, perky, compliant you
one your wife might like, much more
one we will enjoy caring for

The you you like
we don't really care for
too negative, too confronting, too complicated
To simplify:
Too much
Bright, sunny day
heart still in mouth
hole still in chest
life-line frayed,
tethered no more

Other Side

Why don't you come and check it out?
See what it has been like for me
Living with the things you forced upon me
That I didn't want

In my mind, or in my life
I've lived with it from the other side
why don't you come and check it out
from the other chair across from you?

You look at me like there's something wrong
Something lurking inside of me
You think it's your responsibility to control

I often wonder
if you will ever
admit that what you did
mightn't have been
the best thing

For my mind, or for my life
I've lived with it from many sides.
I'd suggest you check it out
from the other chair
across from you.

Us and You

Unified
Straightforward

Always
Notable
Differences

Yarning
Ostentatious
Unilateral

Come Over Here Girl

Come over here girl
Maybe we can work things out
I've seen you looking at me
Checking me out

Been trying to figure out
when you'll come around here again
even though we decided last time
we'd leave it at just friends

You kept coming around
and playing with me
I had to tell you darling
that was not all I could see

I was really thinking of it
as the calm before the storm
waiting for that day you wanted to be alone
or with someone else

Why don't you come around
and spend some time with me
we both know I can live up
to all your fantasies

We've walked this road before
and we both liked what we saw
this time I promise you
I'll stay forever more

Joy

Music
Note
Fingers sliding over the keys
Fingers pressing into the strings

Melody flowing
Harmony sliding in
Voice floating above
Steady rhythm keeping pace below

Heart full
Mind concentrating
Fingers occupied
Soul nurtured

Gratitude

family, family, family
children, wife, brothers,
parents, aunties, Uncles, cousins
friends, work-mates
puppies, chickens
family, family, family

soft, pretty clothes
supportive, comfy shoes
flowers, flowers, flowers

piano, piano, piano,
guitar, voice, harp
zumba, zumba, zumba

privilege, responsibility
privilege, responsibility
privilege, responsibility

musical stitches

how long will the musical stitches last?

I handed my heart to you for safe-keeping

you left it out in the dark
it was kicked about and ripped

she found it out there, in the dark
and held it close while we sung it back together

don't leave it out there again
no more bruises for this beautiful heart

White Privilege

Is it a cruse or a blessing?
BOTH
Those without it have SHAME
embedded in their skin and blood.
Those creamy coconuts, mochal lattes, the
COONS,
the BOINGs, those half-castes.

Did you think my 'half-caste' was your play
thing?
Something to be bargained over, possessed or
owned?

NO!

When the time is right,
we will unite.

My girl has a white mumma with some
Wiradjuri rama rama thrown in.
I will weild that white privilege and bipolar as
the weapons they can be. Only to protect my
babes, and to keep safe all who are in my care.

Together, when the time is right,

we will unite,
and lead our people,
right way, our way.

High aspirations?
Yeah Nah.
Just reverse racism mixed with white Wiradjuri
heritage.

Positive discrimination protected by WHITE
privilege.